Knock Knock Jokes

Funny knock knock jokes for the whole family

Table of Contents

Introduction 1

Knock Knock Jokes 2

Conclusion 65

Introduction

Thank you for choosing this book, full of fun and silly knock knock jokes for the whole family!

In the following pages you will fund hundreds of the funniest, silliest, and most clever knock knock jokes.

I hope you have fun sharing them with your friends and family. Enjoy!

Knock Knock Jokes

Knock knock.

Who's there?

Nobel.

Nobel who?

Nobel… that's why I knocked!

Knock knock.

Who's there?

Tank.

Tank who?

You're welcome!

Knock knock.

Who's there?

Figs.

Figs who?

Figs the doorbell, it's not working!

Knock knock.

Who's there?

Annie.

Annie who?

Annie thing you can do, I can do better!

Knock knock.

Who's there?

Cow says.

Cow says who?

No silly, a cow says moo!

Knock knock.

Who's there?

Says.

Says who?

Says me!

Knock knock.

Who's there?

Lettuce.

Lettuce who?

Lettuce in!

Knock knock.

Who's there?

A little old lady.

A little old lady who?

Oh wow, you can yodel!

Knock knock.

Who's there?

Woo.

Woo who?

Why are you so excited?

Knock knock.

Who's there?

Orange.

Orange who?

Orange you going to let me in?

Knock knock.

Who's there?

Leaf.

Leaf who?

Leaf me alone!

Knock knock.

Who's there?

Annie.

Annie who?

Annie way you can let me in?

Knock knock.

Who's there?

Nana.

Nana who?

Nana your business!

Knock knock.

Who's there?

Iran.

Iran who?

Iran all the way here, let me in!

Knock knock.

Who's there?

Dozen.

Dozen who?

Dozen anyone want to let me in?

Knock knock.

Who's there?

To.

To who?

Actually, it's 'to whom'.

Knock knock.

Who's there?

Europe.

Europe who?

No I'm not, you're a poo!

Knock knock.

Who's there?

Police.

Police who?

Police let me in, it's cold out here!

Knock knock.

Who's there?

Etch.

Etch who?

Bless you!

Knock knock.

Who's there?

Boo.

Boo who?

Awh, don't be sad!

Knock knock.

Who's there?

Theodore.

Theodore who?

Theodore is stuck, would you let me in?

Knock knock.

Who's there?

Stopwatch.

Stopwatch who?

Stopwatch you're doing and let me in!

Knock knock.

Who's there?

Spell.

Spell who?

W.H.O.

Knock knock.

Who's there?

Robin.

Robin who?

Robin you! Give me your money!

Knock knock.

Who's there?

Voodoo.

Voodoo who?

Voodoo you think you are!

Knock knock.

Who's there?

Cash.

Cash who?

No thanks, I prefer almonds.

Knock knock.

Who's there?

Mustache.

Mustache who?

I mustache you a question!

Knock knock.

Who's there?

Mary.

Mary who?

Mary Christmas!

Knock knock.

Who's there?

Alex.

Alex who?

Alex-plain later!

Knock knock.

Who's there?

Iva.

Iva who?

Iva sore hand from knocking!

Knock knock.

Who's there?

Watson.

Watson who?

Watson TV?

Knock knock.

Who's there?

Annie.

Annie who?

Annie one you like!

Knock knock.

Who's there?

Dishes.

Dishes who?

Dishes a really nice place!

Knock knock.

Who's there?

A herd.

A herd who?

A herd you were home, so I came over!

Knock knock.

Who's there?

Norma Lee.

Norma Lee who?

Norma Lee I don't knock on random doors, but here I am!

Knock knock.

Who's there?

Claire.

Claire who?

Claire a path, I'm coming in!

Knock knock.

Who's there?

Roach.

Roach who?

Roach you a text, did you get it?

Knock knock.

Who's there?

Harry.

Harry who?

Harry up and let me in, it's freezing out here!

Knock knock.

Who's there?

Adore.

Adore who?

Adore is between us, so let me in!

Knock knock.

Who's there?

Noah.

Noah who?

Noah cool place we can go hang out?

Knock knock.

Who's there?

Justin.

Justin who?

Justin time for dinner!

Knock knock.

Who's there?

Impatient cow.

Impatient cow wh-

MOOOOOO!

Knock knock.

Who's there?

Abby.

Abby who?

Abby birthday to you!

Knock knock.

Who's there?

Ben.

Ben who?

Ben knocking for 10-minutes, let me in already!

Knock knock.

Who's there?

Al.

Al who?

Al give you a hug if you let me in!

Knock knock.

Who's there?

Amish.

Amish who?

No, you're not a shoe!

Knock knock.

Who's there?

I smell mop.

I smell mop who?

Ew, that's gross!

Knock knock.

Who's there?

Ya.

Ya who?

Yahoo! I'm excited to see you too!

Knock knock.

Who's there?

Honey bee.

Honey bee who?

Honey bee a dear and open the door!

Knock knock.

Who's there?

Mikey.

Mikey who?

Mikey doesn't work, could you unlock the door for me?

Knock knock.

Who's there?

Kanga.

Kanga who?

Actually, it's Kangaroo.

Knock knock.

Who's there?

Olive.

Olive who?

Olive you. Do you love me too?

Knock knock.

Who's there?

Ice cream.

Ice cream who?

Ice cream if you don't let me in!

Knock knock.

Who's there?

Alec.

Alec who?

Alec-tricity! Isn't that a shocker?

Knock knock.

Who's there?

Howl.

Howl who?

Howl you know unless you open the door?

Knock knock.

Who's there?

Says.

Says who?

Says me, that's who!

Knock knock.

Who's there?

Snow.

Snow who?

Snow use asking when you could just open up!

Knock knock.

Who's there?

Stupid.

Stupid who?

Stupid you!

Knock knock.

Who's there?

Water.

Water who?

Water you doing? Just open the door already!

Knock knock.

Who's there?

Amos.

Amos who?

A-mosquito!

Knock knock.

Who's there?

Gorilla.

Gorilla who?

Gorilla me a hamburger!

Knock knock.

Who's there?

Turnip.

Turnip who?

Turnip the volume, I love this song!

Knock knock.

Who's there?

Daisy.

Daisy who?

Daisy me rollin', they hatin'!

Knock knock.

Who's there?

Cargo.

Cargo who?

No, car go beep-beep!

Knock knock.

Who's there?

Alpaca.

Alpaca who?

Alpaca our bags, you get the car!

Knock knock.

Who's there?

Cereal.

Cereal who?

Cereal pleasure to meet you!

Knock knock.

Who's there?

An extraterrestrial.

An extraterrestrial who?

Wait, how many extraterrestrials do you know?!

Knock knock.

Who's there?

Control Freak.

Control Fre-

Okay now you say 'Control Freak who?'

Knock knock.

Who's there?

Yah.

Yah who?

No thanks, I prefer Google.

Knock knock.

Who's there?

Snow.

Snow who?

Snow use, I forgot my name!

Knock knock.

Who's there?

Pecan.

Pecan who?

Pecan someone your own size!

Knock knock.

Who's there?

Dwayne.

Dwayne who?

Dwayne the bathtub, I'm drowning!

Knock knock.

Who's there?

Water.

Water who?

Water your plants, they're starting to die!

Knock knock.

Who's there?

Euripides.

Euripides who?

Euripides jeans, you pay for them!

Knock knock.

Who's there?

Closure.

Closure who?

Closure mouth while you're chewing!

Knock knock.

Who's there?

Owls say.

Owls say who?

Yep, they sure do!

Knock knock.

Who's there?

Ho-ho-ho.

Ho-ho-ho who?

You know, your Santa impression could really use some work...

Knock knock.

Who's there?

Mike Snifferpits.

Mike Snifferpits who?

Come on, how many Mike Snifferpits do you know?!

Knock knock.

Who's there?

Sherlock.

Sherlock who?

Sherlock your door tight!

Knock knock.

Who's there?

Goliath.

Goliath who?

Goliath down, you looketh tired!

Knock knock.

Who's there?

Leena.

Leena who?

Leena little closer and I'll tell you!

Knock knock.

Who's there?

Rhino.

Rhino who?

Rhino every knock knock joke there is!

Knock knock.

Who's there?

Juno.

Juno who?

Juno I love you, right?

Knock knock.

Who's there?

Beets.

Beets who?

Beets me!

Knock knock.

Who's there?

Witches.

Witches who?

Witches the way to the store?

Knock knock.

Who's there?

Broken pencil.

Broken pencil who?

Never mind, there's no point...

Knock knock.

Who's there?

Ice cream soda.

Ice cream soda who?

Ice cream soda whole neighborhood can hear me!

Knock knock.

Who's there?

Egg.

Egg who?

Egg-stremely disappointed that you don't remember me!

Knock knock.

Who's there?

Zany.

Zany who?

Zany body home?

Knock knock.

Who's there?

Teresa.

Teresa who?

Teresa green!

Knock knock.

Who's there?

Amanda.

Amanda who?

Amanda fix your sink!

Knock knock.

Who's there?

Nunya.

Nunya who?

Nunya business!

Knock knock.

Who's there?

Jess.

Jess who?

Jess open the door already!

Knock knock.

Who's there?

Me.

Me who?

Having an identity crisis, are you?

Knock knock.

Who's there?

FBI.

FB-

Hey, we're asking the questions here!

Knock knock.

Who's there?

Cook.

Cook who?

Yeah, you sound crazy!

Knock knock.

Who's there?

Noise.

Noise who?

Noise to see you!

Knock knock.

Who's there?

Aaron.

Aaron who?

Aaron you going to open the door?

Knock knock.

Who's there?

Yukon.

Yukon who?

Yukon say that again!

Knock knock.

Who's there?

Armageddon.

Armageddon who?

Armageddon bored out here, can I come in?

Knock knock.

Who's there?

CD.

CD who?

CD guy on your doorstep?

Knock knock.

Who's there?

Bed.

Bed who?

Bed you can't guess who I am!

Knock knock.

Who's there?

Dishes.

Dishes who?

Dishes the police! Come out with your hands up!

Knock knock.

Who's there?

Ears.

Ears who?

Ears another silly knock knock joke for you!

Knock knock.

Who's there?

Ferdie.

Ferdie who?

Ferdie last time, open the door!

Knock knock.

Who's there?

Ivor.

Ivor who?

Ivor you let me in, or I'm climbing in through the window!

Knock knock.

Who's there?

Lion.

Lion who?

Lion on your doorstep, open up!

Knock knock.

Who's there?

Keanu.

Keanu who?

Keanu let me in? It's cold outside!

Knock knock.

Who's there?

Luke.

Luke who?

Luke through the peephole and find out!

Knock knock.

Who's there?

A little boy.

A little boy who?

A little boy who can't reach the doorbell!

Knock knock.

Who's there?

Fangs.

Fangs who?

Fangs for letting me in!

Knock knock.

Who's there?

Burglar.

Burglar who?

Burglars don't knock!

Knock knock.

Who's there?

Broccoli.

Broccoli who?

Broccoli doesn't have a last name!

Knock knock.

Who's there?

Wooden shoe.

Wooden shoe who?

Wooden shoe like to hear another joke?

Knock knock.

Who's there?

Canoe.

Canoe who?

Canoe come out and play with me?

Knock knock.

Who's there?

Tennis.

Tennis who?

Tennis five plus five.

Knock knock.

Who's there?

Doris.

Doris who?

Doris locked, that's why I'm knocking!

Knock knock.

Who's there?

Isabel.

Isabel who?

Isabel working? I had to knock!

Knock knock.

Who's there?

Leafer.

Leafer who?

Leafer alone!

Knock knock.

Who's there?

Radio.

Radio who?

Radio not, here I come!

Knock knock.

Who's there?

Ida.

Ida who?

Actually, it's pronounced 'Idaho'.

Knock knock.

Who's there?

Hike.

Hike who?

Wow, I didn't know you liked Japanese poetry!

Knock knock.

Who's there?

Howard.

Howard who?

Howard I know!

Knock knock.

Who's there?

Frank.

Frank who?

Frank you for being my friend!

Knock knock.

Who's there?

Vanna.

Vanna who?

Vanna come outside and play?

Conclusion

Thanks again for choosing this book!

I hope you enjoyed these knock knock jokes, and had fun sharing them with your friends and family.

If you enjoyed this book, don't forget to take a look at my other titles available on Amazon and in select retailers!

www.ingramcontent.com/pod-product-compliance
Lightning Source LLC
LaVergne TN
LVHW021735060526
838200LV00052B/3289